Science In Your Life

# MAGNETS
## *Sticking Together*

Wendy Sadler

Raintree

Chicago, Illinois

© 2006 Raintree
Published by Raintree,
a division of Reed Elsevier, Inc.
Chicago, Illinois

Customer Service   888–454–2279

Visit our website at www.raintreelibrary.com

All rights reserved. No part of this publication
may be reproduced or transmitted in any form or
by any means, electronic or mechanical, including
photocopying, recording, taping, or any information
storage and retrieval system, without permission in
writing from the publisher.

Printed by South China Printing Company

10 09 08 07 06
10 9 8 7 6 5 4 3 2 1

**Library of Congress Cataloging-in-
Publication Data**
Sadler, Wendy.
 Magnets : sticking together! / Wendy Sadler.
   p. cm. -- (Science in your life)
 Includes bibliographical references and index.
 ISBN 1-4109-1555-7 (library binding-hardcover) --
ISBN 1-4109-1563-8 (pbk.)
 1. Magnetism--Juvenile literature. 2. Magnets--
Juvenile literature.  I. Title.
 QC753.7.S23 2006
 538'.4--dc22
                          2005014638

**Acknowledgments**
Alamy Images pp. 26 (Brand X Pictures), 11 (Mitch
Diamond), 21 (Rex Argent), 22 (sciencephotos), 15
(Tetra Images), 25 (Thinkstock); Corbis pp. 27 (Mark
M. Lawrence), 16 (Royalty-Free); Getty Images p.17
(PhotoDisc); Harcourt Education Ltd p.10, pp.4, 5, 6,
8, 9, 12, 13, 14, 18, 23, 29 (Tudor Photography);
Science Photo Library p.19 (Simon Fraser).

Cover photograph of a horseshoe magnet
and metal filings reproduced with permission
of Getty/PhotoDisc.

Every effort has been made to contact copyright
holders of any material reproduced in this book.
Any omissions will be rectified in subsequent
printings if notice is given to the publishers.

The paper used to print this book comes from
sustainable resources.

**Disclaimer**
All the Internet addresses (URLs) given in this book
were valid at the time of going to press. However,
due to the dynamic nature of the Internet, some
addresses may have changed, or sites may have
changed or ceased to exist since publication. While
the author and publishers regret any inconvenience
this may cause readers, no responsibility for any
such changes can be accepted by either the author
or the publishers.

An adult should supervise all of the activities in
this book.

# Contents

Any words appearing in the text in bold, **like this**, are explained in the glossary.

# What Are Magnets?

Magnets are special **materials** that can stick to other magnets, or to some metals. Magnets are usually made of metal, but they can be made using other things, too.

Two magnets can either pull together or push apart. A magnet makes a **force** that can be felt by another magnet even if the magnets are not touching. We call this force **magnetism**.

These magnets stick to the fridge door because it is metal.

magnets

There are magnets all around fridge and freezer doors. These help keep the doors shut tightly.

You might not realize it, but magnets and magnetism are all around you!

- You can stick messages to metal **surfaces**, such as fridges, using magnets.
- Magnets are used to make **electricity**.
- Cars and buses have electric **motors** that use magnetism.
- A computer has a flat, magnetic object inside it called the hard disk.

# What Are Magnets Made Of?

Magnetic **material** has a metal called **iron** inside it. Today, magnets are made using a mix of metals.

Some materials—such as plastic, glass, and **aluminum**—can never become magnetic. Magnets that look like they are made of plastic have tiny pieces of iron in them to make them magnetic. If they were only made of plastic, then they would not stick to metal, or to each other.

Magnets come in all shapes and sizes. Do you have any magnets like these in your house?

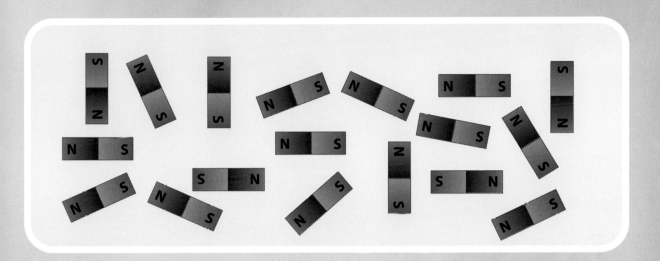

Materials that are magnetic are made up of many tiny magnets called **magnetic domains**. When these are pointing in lots of different directions, the material does not act like a magnet. This means it will not stick to another magnet.

When most of the magnetic domains are pointing in the same direction, the material does act like a magnet. It will stick to another magnet.

# Poles Apart

All magnets have two different ends. These ends are called the north and south poles. If you have two magnets and you bring them close together, the north pole of one will pull toward the south pole of the other.

Poles that are different are attracted to each other, so they pull together. This is called an **attractive force**.

North

South

Magnets come in different shapes, but they all have a north and a south pole.

South

North

If you try to push the north pole of one magnet against the north pole of another magnet, the poles will not want to meet. This means there is a **repulsive force** between them. A repulsive force makes the magnets try to push apart.

These magnets are floating in the air because there is a north pole pushing against a north pole, and then a south pole pushing against a south pole. The magnetic force keeps them apart.

## Magnets in your life!

Find two magnets. Can you hold them in a way that they attract each other and try to pull together? Can you hold them in a way that they repell and push away from each other?

# Sticky Stuff

Magnets can stick to other magnets and to some types of metal. You can use a magnet to find out if objects are magnetic.

## Magnets in your life!

Find a magnet and see which of the following things it will stick to:

- metal kitchen sink
- plastic
- hair
- heating pipe
- drink can
- faucet
- wood.

All of these drink cans will be melted down and used again.

Magnets can be used to sort things. Some drink cans are made of a metal called **steel**, and others are made from **aluminum**. When you **recycle** cans, they need to be sorted into the correct metal so they can be melted down and used again.

If a magnet sticks to a can, then it is made of steel. If a magnet will not stick, then the can is made of aluminum. Some recycling factories use huge magnets to sort magnetic **material** from non-magnetic material.

# Hold On!

When a magnet sticks to a piece of metal, the metal also becomes a magnet! That means the metal has become **magnetized**. Then you can stick another piece of metal to it and make a long magnetic chain.

## Magnets in your life!

Stick a paper clip to a magnet. The paper clip is now magnetized, and you will be able to stick another one to it. How long can you make the dangling chain of paper clips?

Magnets can be useful when you want to hold something in place. You can stick a drawing on a fridge door by putting the paper in between the magnet and the door. The **attractive force** between the magnet and the metal door is strong enough to hold the paper in place.

Can you see the magnets that are used to hold the train cars together?

# Magnetic Earth

Earth is like a giant magnet. There is hot **melted iron** deep inside the Earth. This iron makes lines of **magnetism** around Earth. This is called Earth's **magnetic field**.

If you have a magnet that can swing and point in any direction, it will line itself up with the magnetic field of Earth. This is how a **compass** works.

## Magnets in your life!

You can make a compass by floating the plastic lid of a jar in a bowl of water. Place a bar magnet in the lid. The lid will turn until the magnet lies with one end pointing north and the other pointing south. If the lid floats to the side of the bowl, gently nudge it away.

A magnet always points toward the north pole of Earth as long as no other magnets are close by. Other magnets can push or pull the magnet away from pointing north.

The magnetism in a compass means that you can always find out which way north is.

# Magnetism and Living Things

Most people cannot feel the **magnetic field** of Earth, but some animals can! Some birds fly thousands of miles in the winter and summer to follow the warm weather. We call this **migration**. They can feel the magnetic field of Earth, and they use it to find their way.

These birds find their way by feeling the magnetic field of Earth.

This picture of someone's head was taken using magnetism from an MRI machine.

Doctors can use a machine with a large magnet inside to take a picture of the inside of your body. This helps them look for some illnesses and injuries.

The machine they use is called a magnetic resonance imaging machine, or MRI for short. The magnetism travels through your body and makes pictures to show what is inside.

# Electromagnets

When electricity flows through a wire, it makes a **magnetic field** just like the field from a magnet. This is called an **electromagnet**.

An electromagnet is useful because it can be switched on and off! You could make a simple electromagnet using a battery, some wire, and a nail.

If you wrap wire around an iron nail and connect the wire to a small battery, you can make a simple electromagnet.

wire

nail

battery

Electromagnets can be used in scrapyards to pick up scrap **iron** and old cars. When the magnet is switched on, it picks the scrap up so it can be moved to the place it needs to go. When the magnet is switched off, the **attractive force** also switches off, and the scrap falls down.

A large electromagnet can move scrap metal around a scrapyard.

Electromagnets also can be used as a lock to keep doors closed. The magnets on each side of the door pull toward each other so the door cannot be opened. When you swipe a card or use a special key, the magnet switches off and the door will open.

# Magnets in Motors

An electric **motor** is made of a coil of wire and a magnet. When **electricity** flows through the wire, it makes a **magnetic field**. The magnetic field from the magnet then causes the wire to turn. The motor turns electricity into movement.

magnetic field makes wire turn

horseshoe magnet

electricity flows through the wire and makes a magnetic field

## Where would you be without motors?

Without electric motors there would be no DVD players, food mixers, washing machines, dishwashers, electric trains, CD players, or hairdryers.

This fan uses a motor to turn electricity into a spinning movement. When the motor turns, it makes the blades of the fan turn. The blades push air forward to cool you down.

# Making Electricity

Magnets can also be used to make **electricity**. If you move a magnet over a wire, you make a small amount of electricity flow through the wire.

Some bicycles have a machine called a **dynamo** fixed to the wheels. As the bicycle wheels turn, they make a magnet turn inside coils of wire in the dynamo. This makes enough electricity to power the bicycle lights!

This is a wind-up radio. You wind it up by hand. As it unwinds, a magnet turns inside a coil of wire. This makes enough electricity to power the radio.

Most of the electricity we use every day is made using magnets. Power stations burn oil to heat water, which makes steam. This steam has enough **energy** to turn large coils of wire around huge magnets. This makes the electricity that is carried along wires to people's homes.

We use electricity for many things such as heating, lighting, and cooking. Electricity powers our computers and televisions. What would we do without electricity?

# Magnets and Sound

We use speakers to listen to sound when we play music or watch television. A coil of wire inside the speaker carries electric **signals**. There is a magnet around the wire. When **electricity** flows through the wire, the magnet around it pushes and pulls the wire in the same pattern as the electric signal. These pushes and pulls make the speaker **vibrate.** This vibration is the sound that we hear.

coil of wire

–

+

electric signals

speaker cone vibrates to make sound

When you use speakers to listen to music or the television, you are using magnets to turn electric signals into sound.

Magnets are also used to record sound. Inside a microphone there is a moving coil of wire and a magnet. When you make a noise into the microphone, the vibration of your voice makes the coil move. The coil moves inside the magnet, and this makes electric signals that travel through the wires to be recorded.

A microphone turns sound into electric signals. A speaker turns the electric signals back into sounds.

# Magnetic Information

Magnetic **material** can store information as a pattern. If you look at the back of a credit card, you will find a black strip. Although the card is made of plastic, this part of the card is actually a magnetic code.

When you pay for something in a store, the card passes through a special machine. The machine can read the magnetic code so that it can tell who is paying.

The black strip on this card has a magnetic code.

If you record a television program on a videotape, you are storing sounds and pictures as magnetic patterns. Computers also have a magnetic disk inside that stores lots of information.

This is the magnetic disk inside a computer. This is where information is stored and kept safe.

### Imagine life without magnets

Magnets help us save information and then play it back. Without magnets you would not be able to record your favorite TV program or store information on your computer.

# Facts About Magnets

In the United States none of the coins is magnetic, but magnetic ink is used to print bank notes! Can you find out which ones are magnetic?

One woman in the United States has collected over 35,000 fridge magnets. She must have a very large fridge!

The strength of a magnet is measured in Tesla (T) or Gauss (G).

Grapes are slightly repelled by very strong magnets called rare-earth magnets!

There is a magnetic fluid called ferrofluid that has tiny magnetic particles mixed in it.

The word "magnet" comes from Magnesia in Greece where they were first discovered.

# Find Out More

You can find out more about science in everyday life by talking to your teacher or parents. Your local library will also have books that can help. You will find the answers to many of your questions in this book. If you want to know more, you can use other books and the Internet.

## More books to read

Cooper, Chris. *Science Answers: Magnetism.* Chicago: Heinemann Library, 2003.

Hunter, Rebecca. *Discovering Science: Electricity and Magnetism.* Chicago: Raintree, 2003.

Parker, Steve. *Science Files: Electricity and Magnetism.* Chicago: Heinemann Library, 2004.

## Using the Internet

Explore the Internet to find out more about magnets. Try using a search engine such as www.yahooligans.com or www.internet4kids.com, and type in keywords such as "**dynamo**," "**magnetic field**," and "**motor**."

**aluminum** light metal that magnets will not stick to. Some drink cans are made of aluminum.

**attractive force** power that pulls two things together

**compass** machine with a small magnet inside that always points to north. You can use a compass to help find your way.

**dynamo** machine that you might find on a bike. When the wheels turn, the movement makes electricity, usually for light.

**electricity** form of energy that can be used to make things run. Computers and televisions run using electricity.

**electromagnet** magnet that can be switched on and off using electricity

**energy** power to make things work. You need energy to get up and walk or run around.

**iron** type of metal that is magnetic and can be made into a magnet

**magnetic domain** small magnetic area inside something

**magnetic field** area around a magnet where the force of the magnet pushes and pulls

**magnetism** having the properties of a magnet

**magnetize** when a metal becomes a magnet

**material** something that objects are made from

**melted** when a solid is heated up and turned into a liquid

**migration** movement from one area to another. Some birds migrate in the winter to find warmer places to live.

**motor** machine that makes things move

**recycle** use the material from old things to make something new

**repulsive force** magnetic force that pushes two things apart

**signal** sign or message

**steel** type of metal that magnets will stick to. Some drink cans are made of steel.

**surface** top or outside part of an object

**vibrate** move up and down or backward and forward very quickly

# Index